Natural History Mysteries

Anita Ganeri

Illustrated by Amerigo Pinelli

OXFORD
UNIVERSITY PRESS

Contents

Mystery or History?

Is there really a monster **lurking** in Loch Ness? Do giant apemen actually exist? What happened to the lost city of Atlantis? Are UFOs really alien spacecraft or just tricks of the light?

For hundreds of years, people have been puzzled by mysterious creatures, places and objects. Sometimes there is not enough **evidence** to prove what they are, or whether they exist.

People have tried to find these answers for years. But are there some mysteries that just cannot be solved? Read on, and make up your own mind ...

FACT OR FICTION?

For each mystery, you will see a box like this one. It will help you think about which parts of the mystery are facts, and which parts have been made up.

Creatures of the Night

July 1924, Muddy River, Washington State, United States of America (USA)

It was midnight. Five gold miners were asleep in their cabin in the woods. Suddenly a loud, thudding noise woke them up. It sounded as if someone, or *something*, was throwing rocks at the cabin walls ...

The miners peeked out through the window. They could just make out three huge, apelike creatures, covered in shaggy hair. The creatures were trying to break down the heavy log door. Next, they were up on the roof. The miners picked up their guns and opened fire but the attacks went on all night.

The next day, the miners packed up and left the cabin. What were the extraordinary creatures that they had seen?

Apeman Sightings

The apelike creatures that the miners saw became known as 'Bigfoot', because of the huge footprints they left behind. Many other apemen have been seen all over the world. One of the most famous apemen is the Yeti, or 'Abominable Snowman', from Asia.

FACT OR FICTION?

There are many ideas about what the Yeti and Bigfoot might really be. Are they a new type of giant ape? Or are they long-lost humans? Do they exist at all? It is still a mystery.

Looking for clues

No one has caught an apeman yet, but here are some more pieces of evidence. Sadly, it seems that some, or all, of these are fakes.

Exhibit A: Footprints and tracks

Exhibit B: **Scalps** and skins

Exhibit C: Photographs

Exhibit D: Films and videos

Something in the Water

June 1972, Loch Ness, Scotland

An American scientist, Dr Robert Rines, was having tea with his wife and friends. They were staying in a cottage on the shore of Loch Ness. After tea, one of Dr Rines's friends went outside. Suddenly, he cried out. "Come quickly and bring the binoculars!" he shouted.

Dr Rines rushed down to the lake and peered through the binoculars. He could not believe his eyes. Moving slowly across the water was a huge, round hump, about the size of an upturned boat. As Rines watched, the hump changed direction and headed straight towards him. Then it vanished into the lake.

Who or what did the hump belong to? Dr Rines had no doubt. There was only one creature it could be – the Loch Ness Monster.

Prehistoric Monster

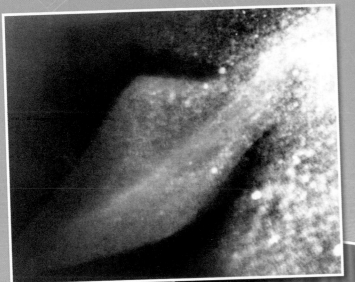

A few months later, Dr Rines came back to Loch Ness to hunt for the monster. He set up cameras under the water to **snap** anything that moved. One photo seemed to show a diamond-shaped flipper that might belong to a large swimming creature.

FACT OR FICTION?

Some people think that the monster could be a Plesiosaur. Plesiosaurs were reptiles with long necks that lived underwater during the time of the dinosaurs. They are thought to have died out about 70 million years ago.

More lake monsters

Loch Ness is not the only lake where monsters are thought to lurk. Similar creatures have been spotted in many lakes around the world. Here is a quick spotter's guide:

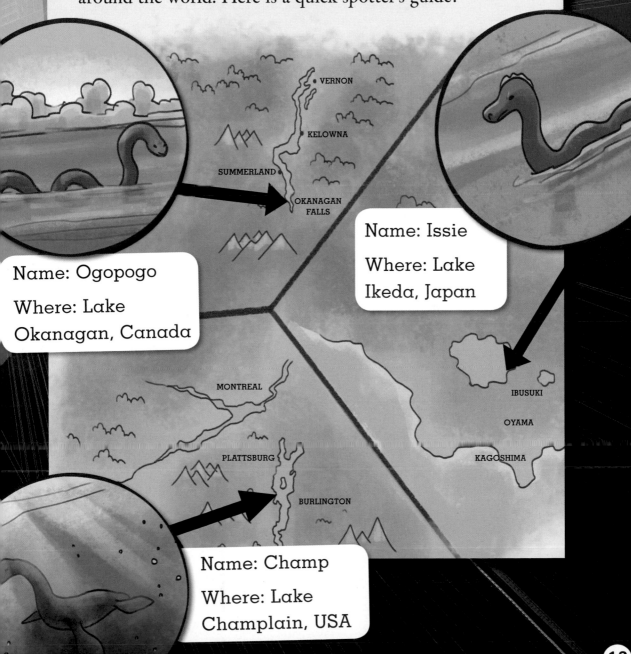

Name: Ogopogo

Where: Lake Okanagan, Canada

Name: Issie

Where: Lake Ikeda, Japan

Name: Champ

Where: Lake Champlain, USA

Sunken City

About 10000 BCE, Atlantic Ocean

Around 12000 years ago, legend says, a rich and powerful island lay in the Atlantic Ocean. It was called Atlantis. Its main city was built in the shape of a circle and stood on top of a hill. Here, the king lived in a magnificent palace, surrounded by gardens. There was also a fabulous temple dedicated to the sea god, Poseidon. It was covered in silver, gold and other precious metals. Behind the city was a great plain, where farmers grew food.

Then, one day, violent earthquakes and floods hit Atlantis. In the space of a day and a night, the island vanished beneath the waves. No sign of Atlantis has ever been found. Today, no one knows if the island ever existed at all.

Lost at Sea

All our information about Atlantis comes from Plato, an ancient Greek writer. But Plato's report was written thousands of years after Atlantis is supposed to have disappeared.

FACT OR FICTION?

In about 1650 BCE, a huge volcanic eruption blew apart the island Thera, near the Greek island of Crete. Some people think that it also destroyed Atlantis, or that Thera itself was Atlantis, even though Thera wasn't in the Atlantic Ocean.

ATLANTIC OCEAN

?

AFRICA

SOUTH AMERICA

N
W E
S

MISSING KINGDOM!

Name: Lyonesse

Last known address: Cornwall, England – in the sea, about ten kilometres off Land's End

Last seen: 5th century CE

Legend says:

- Lyonesse was a great kingdom that linked Cornwall to France.
- It was **submerged** under a huge wave.
- Only one man survived. He rode to safety on his horse.

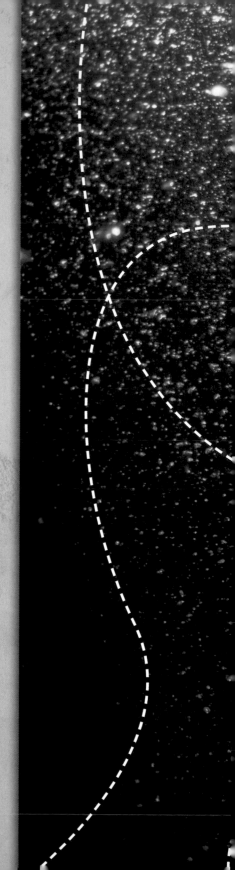

Flight to Nowhere

December 1945, Atlantic Ocean, off the coast of Florida, USA

At two o'clock on the afternoon of 5th December, five US Navy bombers of Flight 19 took off from Fort Lauderdale in Florida. They were on a training **mission** meant to last two hours. The weather was good over the Atlantic Ocean. At first, everything went as planned ...

The first signs of trouble came at quarter to four. There were problems with the planes' **compasses** and the radios were not working properly. Soon the pilots realised that they were hopelessly lost. A last radio message was heard at seven o'clock and two seaplanes went out to search for the missing planes.

The search continued for another five days but no sign of Flight 19 was ever found. The five planes had simply vanished in a mysterious stretch of ocean, known as the Bermuda Triangle.

Missing Planes and ships

The Bermuda Triangle is part of the Atlantic Ocean between Bermuda, Miami and Puerto Rico. People claim that many craft have gone missing here, although there is not much evidence to back this up.

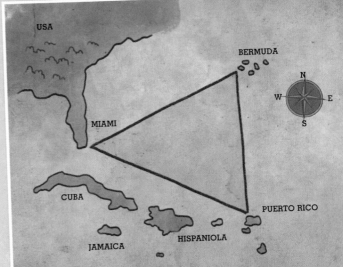

FACT OR FICTION?

Why did the Flight 19 bombers disappear? Perhaps the pilots made a mistake or bad weather was to blame? It has even been suggested that the planes were kidnapped by aliens!

The Daily Mystery

Missing crew on mystery ship

A mysterious ship was spotted yesterday by the crew of the *Dei Gratia*.

Three sailors rowed over and searched the ship, named the *Mary Celeste*, from top to bottom. Everything looked normal – there was even a meal laid out. But the ship was deserted. The whole crew had vanished without a trace.

Alien Landing

July 1947, Roswell, New Mexico, USA

The man stared down at the ghostly body on the ground. Shivers ran down his spine. He had never seen anything like it before. The creature was deathly pale, with scaly skin and huge eyes. It was not human, but what else could it be? All around lay chunks of twisted metal. Something large had smashed to the ground.

Days before, people had seen strange lights in the sky above Roswell. One of the lights seemed to have come crashing down to the ground. Was it an Unidentified Flying Object (UFO)? If so, was the creature an alien? The government wanted to keep the crash site a secret but rumours soon spread that a 'flying saucer' had landed.

The metal found at Roswell turned out to have come from a **weather balloon** and not from a flying saucer. As for the alien? There is no evidence that it was ever there at all.

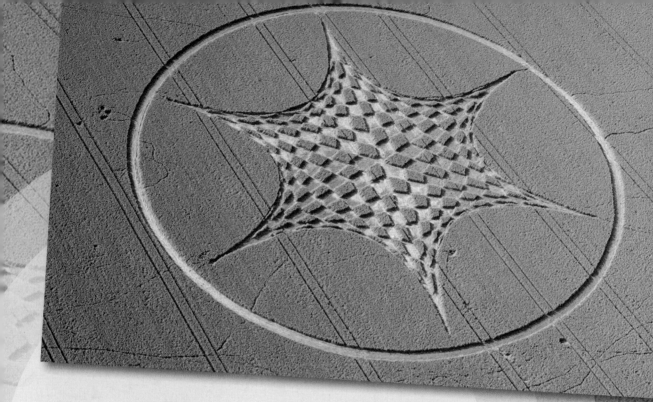

Crop circles

Crop circles are circular patterns which mysteriously appear in fields of crops. Some people think they are landing sites for alien spacecraft. We know now that most of them are a **hoax**.

FACT OR FICTION?

Some photographs of UFOs have turned out to be deliberate fakes. In 1962, two boys painted saucer shapes on a sheet of glass and took a photo through it. Many people were fooled into believing that the photo was real.

Circles of Stone

About 2600–1600 BCE, Salisbury Plain, Wiltshire, England

Thousands of years ago, an extraordinary **monument** was built on Salisbury Plain. It is called Stonehenge and was built in stages over hundreds of years. It is made from giant stones which stand upright in circles. Some of the stones are enormous. They had to be dragged all the way from Wales, around 250 kilometres away, using rollers and leather ropes.

Stonehenge must have been important, but no one is sure what it was used for. Some experts think that it was a temple where people came to **worship** the Sun and Moon. Or perhaps it was a giant calendar that told people the time of year? Maybe it was a place where important rulers were buried? Nobody knows.

Mysterious Designs

Once, people thought that giants or demons built Stonehenge! Experts now think that people travelled from all over Britain to help with the building work.

Another huge and mysterious design can be found in the Nazca Desert in Peru.

Hi!

I'm visiting the famous Nazca Lines. These giant lines across the desert were made by the Nazca people about 1500 years ago. Some of the lines are straight but others are made into the shape of animals. No one knows why they were made.

Wow!

Luke Baxter

33 Old Road

Anytown

UK

FACT OR FICTION?

Some people think the Nazca people drew the lines as messages to their gods. Another idea is that they were landing places for alien spacecraft.

Our world holds so many mysteries, and different ideas about what they mean. Whatever answers you decide are right, there are more questions out there ...

Glossary

compasses: instruments that show which direction you are travelling in – they have a needle which always points North

evidence: facts or information that give us a reason to believe something

hoax: a trick, an attempt to make people believe something which is not true

lurking: waiting or hiding somewhere

mission: an important job that someone is sent to do

monument: a statue or building that reminds people of a famous person or event

scalps: the skin on the top of your head, sometimes taken by warriors from victims in battle

snap: take a photograph

submerged: put under water

weather balloon: a hot-air balloon sent into the atmosphere to measure weather conditions

worship: praise or respect a god or gods

Index

About the Author

I was born in India but came to the United Kingdom on a plane when I was only one. Today, I live in northern England with my husband, children and three dogs. I work at home in my office and the biggest mystery in my life is how my computer works.

Are the mysteries in this book real? Some people don't believe in UFOs, yetis or monsters. But if you're standing on the misty shores of Loch Ness, and you see a black shape in the water, you might just change your mind.

Greg Foot, Series Editor

I've loved science ever since the day I took my papier mâché volcano into school. I filled it with far too much baking powder, vinegar and red food colouring, and WHOOSH! I covered the classroom ceiling in red goo. Now I've got the best job in the world: I present TV shows for the BBC, answer kids' science questions on YouTube, and make huge explosions on stage at festivals!

Working on TreeTops inFact has been great fun. There are so many brilliant books, and guess what ... they're all packed full of awesome facts! What's your favourite?